LEVEL 2 SCIENCE
LET'S READ AND FIND OUT

A PANDEMIC IS

WORLDWIDE

BY SARAH L. THOMSON • ILLUSTRATED BY TAIA MORLEY

HARPER
An Imprint of HarperCollinsPublishers

Special thanks to Dr. Eben Kenah, Associate Professor of Biostatistics
at the Ohio State University, for his valuable assistance.

The Let's-Read-and-Find-Out Science book series was originated by Dr. Franklyn M. Branley, Astronomer Emeritus
and former Chairman of the American Museum of Natural History–Hayden Planetarium, and was formerly
coedited by him and Dr. Roma Gans, Professor Emeritus of Childhood Education, Teachers College, Columbia University.
Text and illustrations for each of the books in the series are checked for accuracy by an expert in the relevant field.
For more information about Let's-Read-and-Find-Out Science books, write to HarperCollins Children's Books,
195 Broadway, New York, NY 10007, or visit our website at www.letsreadandfindout.com.

Let's Read-and-Find-Out Science® is a trademark of HarperCollins Publishers.

A Pandemic Is Worldwide
Text copyright © 2022 by Sarah L. Thomson
Illustrations by Taia Morley
Illustrations copyright © 2022 by HarperCollins Publishers
All rights reserved. Manufactured in Italy.
No part of this book may be used or reproduced in any manner whatsoever without written permission
except in the case of brief quotations embodied in critical articles and reviews. For information address
HarperCollins Children's Books, a division of HarperCollins Publishers, 195 Broadway, New York, NY 10007.
www.harpercollinschildrens.com

Library of Congress Control Number: 2021936544
ISBN 978-0-06-308626-5 (trade bdg.) — ISBN 978-0-06-308632-6 (pbk.)

The artist used a combination of watercolor and digital techniques to create the illustrations for this book.

Designed by Elaine Lopez-Levine

21 22 23 24 25 RTLO 10 9 8 7 6 5 4 3 2 1 ❖ First Edition

R0461794690

For everyone who got us through! —S.L.T.

*For all our local librarians who keep our
public libraries vital, especially in COVID times* —T.M.

Everybody gets sick now and then—
maybe with a runny nose or a sore
throat, an upset stomach or an
aching head.

Sometimes a lot of people get sick at once. If many people in your school or
your town or your state get the same disease at the same time, that's an outbreak.

Sometimes an outbreak grows beyond the town or the state where it started. If a lot of people in one country or even a few countries catch a particular disease, that's an epidemic. If the disease spreads all over the world, that's a pandemic.

Pan means "all." *Demic* means "of or about the people." A pandemic is something happening to all people.

11

A disease that spreads from person to person—the kind of disease that can create a pandemic—is caused by bacteria or viruses.

These tiny beings can get inside your body, often through your mouth or your nose or your eyes or a cut in your skin. Once they're inside, they might make you sick.

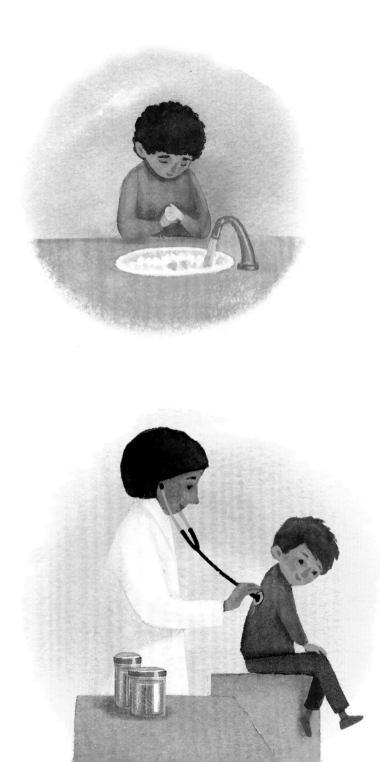

Washing hands, covering cuts and scrapes, and staying away from people who are sick can keep us healthy.

If we do catch bacteria or a virus, our bodies can usually fight it off.

Doctors may give us medicine that will help.

But every now and then a new kind of bacteria or virus appears. Because the sickness is new, our bodies don't know how to fight it. There's no medicine that can cure it, at least not at first. If this new virus or bacteria spreads easily, it may cause a pandemic—like the one that reached the shores of the Black Sea in the 1340s.

People there began to get sick from the bacteria that caused bubonic plague. Later, people called this sickness the Black Death.

Traders who sailed from the Black Sea to Italy brought the plague with them. Rulers of some Italian cities declared that all newcomers must stay outside their city walls for forty days—a *quarentino*.

They hoped this would keep everyone safe from the new disease. *Quarentino* became the English word *quarantine*. To quarantine people who are sick or who may be sick means to keep them away from others.

The *quarentino* could not keep the Black Death from reaching the rest of Europe, and Asia and Africa too. But it showed that people were beginning to understand how a pandemic can spread and what can be done to stop it.

Starting in the late 1400s, people began to sail from Europe to North and South America. These invaders brought a virus that causes smallpox, a sickness that was old to them but new to the people of the Americas.

We think that eight or nine of every ten Native Americans died after Europeans came. They were killed by war, slavery, starvation, and disease—especially smallpox.

The end to the smallpox pandemic began in 1796. That was when a doctor named Edward Jenner created the first true vaccine.

A vaccine does not cure someone who is sick. It stops them from catching a sickness in the first place.

If someone cannot catch a particular disease, they are immune to it. People who took Edward Jenner's vaccine were immune to smallpox. Over time, more and more people became immune, and the smallpox virus slowly died out.

A century and a half after Edward Jenner's vaccine, in 1928, a doctor named Alexander Fleming noticed that one of the dishes in his laboratory had gone moldy.

That mold had done something remarkable. It had killed the bacteria around it. Fleming's mold led to a powerful new medicine called penicillin. It was the first antibiotic, something that can kill bacteria inside the body.

23

Today we have many different antibiotics. We have vaccines that make people immune to certain viruses or bacteria. And we understand a lot about how to stop disease from spreading. Pandemics are rare, but they can still happen.

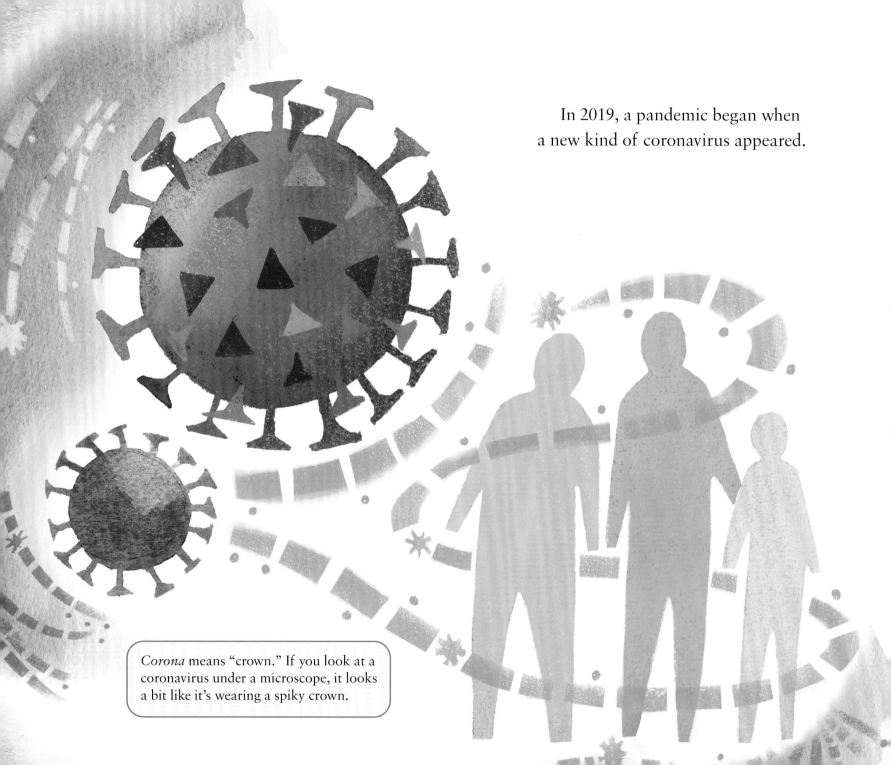

In 2019, a pandemic began when a new kind of coronavirus appeared.

Corona means "crown." If you look at a coronavirus under a microscope, it looks a bit like it's wearing a spiky crown.

Coronaviruses usually cause colds. But this new one causes a sickness called COVID-19. Some people with COVID-19 don't get sick at all. But others have coughs and fevers. It may become hard for them to breathe.

Many people are weak and have no energy. Some can't taste or smell anything.

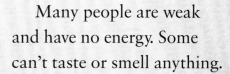

CO stands for "corona." VI stands for "virus." D stands for "disease." The 19 is because the virus first appeared in people in 2019.

27

The coronavirus spreads through drops of saliva and mucus. When sick people cough or sneeze or sing or yell or even breathe, droplets fly out of their mouths and noses. If someone breathes the droplets in, that person may become sick too. During the pandemic, people wore masks to keep this from happening.

The virus also spreads by getting on our hands. If we touch our faces, it can slip into our eyes or noses or mouths. So people washed their hands—a lot! Soap doesn't just wash the coronavirus away. It actually kills the virus by ripping it apart.

Stop the COVID-19 Spread

Simple choices like staying home as much as you can and wearing a mask when you go out can help slow the spread of a disease like COVID-19.

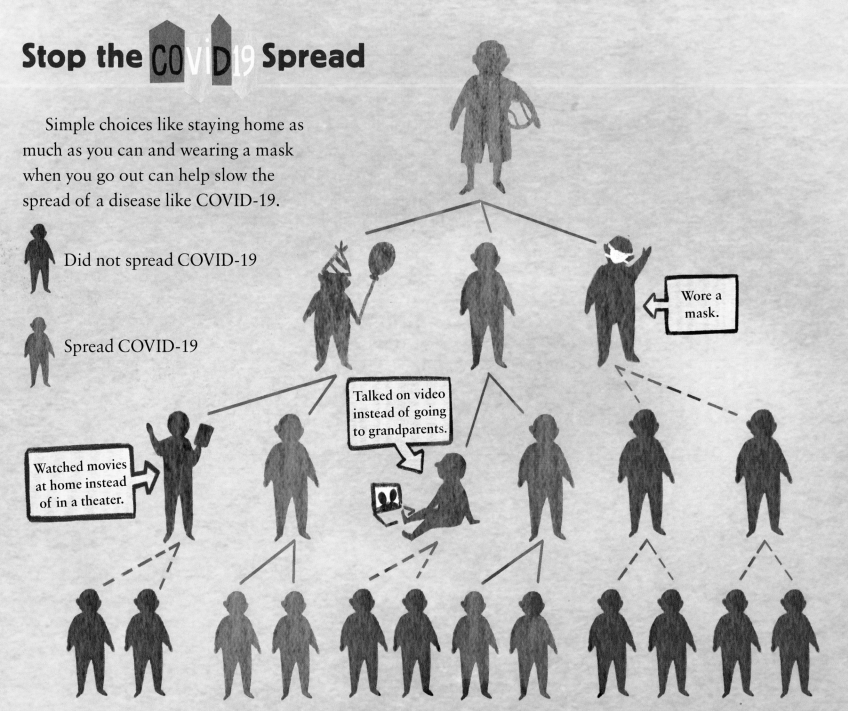

Did not spread COVID-19

Spread COVID-19

Wore a mask.

Watched movies at home instead of in a theater.

Talked on video instead of going to grandparents.

People kept away from others as much as they could so that the virus would not spread from sick people to healthy ones. Schools were shut. Many grown-ups did their jobs from home.

Slowing the spread of COVID-19 gave doctors and scientists time to find vaccines. COVID-19 might never go away. But vaccines made most people immune.

Grown-ups could go back to work. Schools could open again. Children could go to birthday parties and playgrounds and visit family. Everyone who wore a mask or washed their hands or stayed home until it was safe helped bring about the day when the pandemic was over at last.

33

Glossary

Antibiotic: a medicine that kills bacteria

Bacteria: small living things that may cause sickness if they get inside a body

Epidemic: a sickness that many people in a state or country or a few countries catch in a short time

Immune: cannot catch a particular sickness

Mucus: a slimy coating in the nose and lungs (and other places in the body as well)

Outbreak: a sickness that many people in a certain area catch in a short time

Pandemic: a sickness that many people all over the world catch

Vaccine: a medicine that keeps you from catching a particular virus

Viruses: tiny things (usually smaller than bacteria) that can cause sickness if they get inside a body. Viruses are not alive in the same way that people, animals, and bacteria are, but they act like living things in many ways.

Handwashing Diagram

We can stop the spread of viruses and bacteria by washing our hands for at least 20 seconds. Time this by singing the A-B-C song (not too fast!). (Hand sanitizer does the same thing, but soap works better.)

1. Get hands wet. Then turn off the water so you don't waste it.

2. Rub the soap to make lots of bubbles. "A-B-C-D . . ."

3. Rub the palm of one hand on the back of the other. Get between the fingers. "E-F-G . . ." Switch hands. "H-I-J-K . . ."

4. Wash each thumb. "L-M-N-O-P . . ."

5. Scratch the palm of one hand with the fingernails of the other, then switch hands. (This cleans under the nails.) "Q-R-S-T-U-V . . ."

6. Turn the water back on and rinse your hands. "W-X-Y and Z!"

7. Dry your hands.

35

Some Pandemics of the Past

100

500

1000

1300

1500

Antonine Plague
(probably measles
and smallpox)
AD 165–180
Around 5 million died

Justinian's Plague
AD 541–543
30–50 million died
Justinian's plague was
part of the first bubonic
plague pandemic.

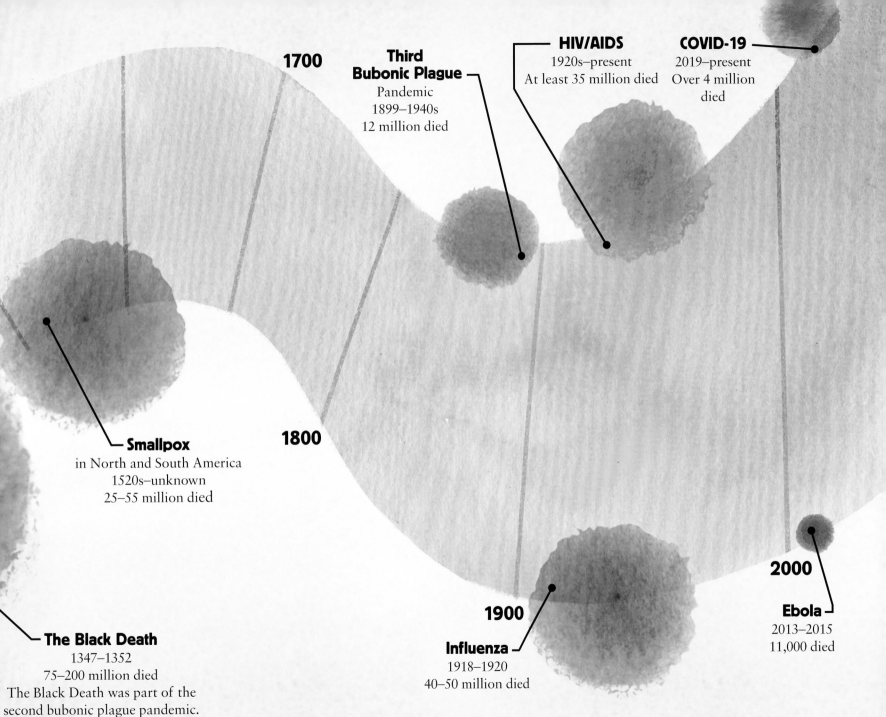

1700

1800

1900

2000

Third Bubonic Plague
Pandemic
1899–1940s
12 million died

HIV/AIDS
1920s–present
At least 35 million died

COVID-19
2019–present
Over 4 million died

Smallpox
in North and South America
1520s–unknown
25–55 million died

Influenza
1918–1920
40–50 million died

Ebola
2013–2015
11,000 died

The Black Death
1347–1352
75–200 million died
The Black Death was part of the second bubonic plague pandemic.

Be sure to look for all of these books in the Let's-Read-and-Find-Out Science series:

The Human Body:
How Many Teeth?
I'm Growing!
My Feet
My Five Senses
My Hands
Sleep Is for Everyone
What's for Lunch?

Plants and Animals:
Animals in Winter
The Arctic Fox's Journey
Baby Whales Drink Milk
Big Tracks, Little Tracks
Bugs Are Insects
Dinosaurs Big and Small
Ducks Don't Get Wet
Fireflies in the Night
From Caterpillar to Butterfly
From Seed to Pumpkin
From Tadpole to Frog
How Animal Babies Stay Safe
How a Seed Grows
A Nest Full of Eggs
Starfish
Super Marsupials
Thump Goes the Rabbit
A Tree Is a Plant
What Lives in a Shell?
What's Alive?
What's It Like to Be a Fish?
Where Are the Night Animals?
Where Do Chicks Come From?

The World Around Us:
Air Is All Around You
The Big Dipper
Clouds
Is There Life in Outer Space?
Pop!
Snow Is Falling
Sounds All Around
The Sun and the Moon
What Makes a Shadow?

The Human Body:
A Drop of Blood
Germs Make Me Sick!
Hear Your Heart
A Pandemic Is Worldwide
The Skeleton Inside You
What Happens to a Hamburger?
Why I Sneeze, Shiver, Hiccup, and Yawn
Your Skin and Mine

Plants and Animals:
Almost Gone
Ant Cities
Be a Friend to Trees
Chirping Crickets
Corn Is Maize
Dolphin Talk
Honey in a Hive
How Do Apples Grow?
How Do Birds Find Their Way?
Life in a Coral Reef
Look Out for Turtles!
Milk from Cow to Carton
An Octopus Is Amazing
Penguin Chick
Sharks Have Six Senses
Snakes Are Hunters
Spinning Spiders
What Color Is Camouflage?
Who Eats What?
Who Lives in an Alligator Hole?
Why Do Leaves Change Color?
Why Frogs Are Wet
Wiggling Worms at Work
Zipping, Zapping, Zooming Bats

Dinosaurs:
Did Dinosaurs Have Feathers?
Digging Up Dinosaurs
Dinosaur Bones
Dinosaur Tracks
Dinosaurs Are Different
Fossils Tell of Long Ago
My Visit to the Dinosaurs
Pinocchio Rex and Other Tyrannosaurs
What Happened to the Dinosaurs?
Where Did Dinosaurs Come From?

Space:
Floating in Space
The International Space Station
Mission to Mars
The Moon Seems to Change
The Planets in Our Solar System
The Sky Is Full of Stars
The Sun
What Makes Day and Night
What the Moon Is Like

Weather and the Seasons:
Down Comes the Rain
Droughts
Feel the Wind
Flash, Crash, Rumble, and Roll
Hurricane Watch
Sunshine Makes the Seasons
Tornado Alert
What Makes a Blizzard?
What Will the Weather Be?

Our Earth:
Archaeologists Dig for Clues
Earthquakes
Flood Warning
Follow the Water from Brook to Ocean
How Deep Is the Ocean?
How Mountains Are Made
In the Rainforest
Let's Go Rock Collecting
Oil Spill!
Volcanoes
What Happens to Our Trash?
What's So Bad About Gasoline?
Where Do Polar Bears Live?
Why Are the Ice Caps Melting?
You're Aboard Spaceship Earth

The World Around Us:
Day Light, Night Light
Energy Makes Things Happen
Forces Make Things Move
Gravity Is a Mystery
How a City Works
How People Learned to Fly
How to Talk to Your Computer
Light Is All Around Us
Phones Keep Us Connected
Running on Sunshine
Simple Machines
Switch On, Switch Off
What Is the World Made Of?
What Makes a Magnet?
Where Does the Garbage Go?